Celtic Quilt Designs

Adapted by Philomena Durcan Wiechec

CELTIC INTERLACE DESIGNS FOR QUILTS

Celtic art is very old. From the 6th to the 12th century, A.D., Celtic art found expression and flowered in Gospel books, stone carvings — mostly on tomb stones, and metal carvings — most notable being the Tara Brooch and the Ardagh Chalice. It was mainly in the Gospel books that the amazingly beautiful art grew and left its heritage for us all. Interlace was one variation of the many Celtic art forms that flourished. As Christianity spread in Ireland and England, demand for Gospel books rose, and so did the desire to embellish them. Most of these old books have been lost or destroyed. The most prominent remaining one is the Book of Kells, now preserved at Trinity College, Dublin, Ireland. This lovely book of Celtic art with its intricate interlace patterns is what led to my inspiration for the quilt designs.

When I was first asked to make a friendship block, I decided I would express my own self, which is Irish. I had seen some Celtic embroidery designs in a Dublin, Ireland store that I felt would allow me to express myself. I selected two different designs for the two requests and managed to amateurishly finish them. The delighted response was, no doubt, the beginning of the making of my first quilt. For this quilt I selected the lovely "Celtic friendship rings." My beginnings and involvement in quilting have been splendidly told by Anne Wittels in the August 1978 issue of Quilt World which you may want to read.

For a while it appeared that I might be a "one-quilt maker." However, with the urging and support of my new-found friends, Pat Gardner and Marmie Schraub, and the other members of the Sew n Sew club, I finally got started in the making of another quilt. Their enthusiasm to my first adaptation of Celtic design, and to my use of color, urged me on. After that first adaptation there was an evolution to new and more intricate Celtic designs. When four new designs were formed, my friends suggested I make a sampler quilt. Happily, and again with their prodding and support, the enclosed designs evolved and so did the idea for making this book.

As with all new projects, the beginning was clumsy and tortuous. I first started by making templates for the designs. However, Pat and Marmie suggested I try the "bias applique" method. Even with this method the process was a struggle. It was then that Marmie told me of her method of making bias. The more bias I made, the easier and faster that bias applique became. I am now recommending that others try this simplified bias applique technique, as, surely, there are an infinite number of new designs yet to be discovered for which this technique can be used.

In addition to making beautiful quilts, the same designs can also be used to make trapunto and stained glass applique. I'm sure many of you will experiment with many more applications, and I hope you will enjoy the designs.

*May your sorrows be patched
and your joys be quilted.*

Philomena Wiechec

INSTRUCTIONS

Celtic interlace is noted for its "under and over" condition, which, once started, must be consistent throughout the whole design. There is another hard and fast rule for making Celtic interlace. At any one point in the design, no more than two lines may cross.

The preferred way to do these designs is by "bias applique." A steel or aluminum bar is used for pressing the bias. This bar will be called the "bias bar."* Marmie cut through the closed ends of a Dritz sewing gauge. Then she rounded and smoothed the ends to make two bias bars — one ¼" and one ⅜." I found that an 18" strip of thermoplastic heating wire served me just as well. I used a ¹⁄₁₆" thick, ⁵⁄₁₆" wide, and 18" long bar which helped me make ⅜" bias for my designs. Use your imagination for selecting your own bias bar; however, be sure the material you choose can resist the heat of an iron and does not have edges sharp enough to damage the material.

The "Marmie" method makes bias applique easy. She has kindly granted permission for me to share her method with you.

1. *Mark true bias lines, one inch apart, on fabric to be used.*
2. *Cut out the marked 1⅛" strips, some of which should be 60" long.*
3. *Fold one strip in half with cut edges together and right sides out.*
4. *Machine sew the folded strip about ⅛" from the edges. You now have a tube strip ready to be ironed.*
5. *Finish remaining strips just as above.*
6. *Place bias bar into tube strip and steam press down the seamed material over the flat side of the bias bar. Reverse to other side and steam press again. Push the bias bar farther into the tube strip and press until the whole strip is pressed.*

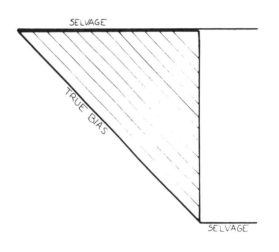

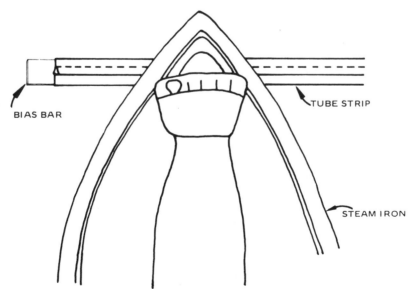

7. *Press all other machine sewn strips as above.*

* See back page

3

MAKING WHOLE DESIGNS

Because of limitation of space, only half of the design is shown in the book. You must assemble the whole design yourself. In this book I show a little more than half the design. When making the whole design, eliminate all of the design over the designated half design. There are two ways to make the full design:

1. *By tracing on tracing paper.*
   a. *Trace the half design on a 16½" square piece of tracing paper. Use a fine black felt pen. Rotate (do not flip!) the tracing paper 180 degrees counterclockwise, and trace the design again so that you will now have a whole design. The reason for the rotation is to make the "over and under" consistent throughout the whole design.*
2. *By Xerox copying.*
   a. *Make two copies of the half design. Cut the paper exactly to the lines marking the half design. Rotate one of the half designs again and tape together.*

You now have a whole design. The tracing paper copy can be used directly to make a tracing onto fabric.

TRACING DESIGN TO FABRIC

To make a tracing onto fabric, tape a tracing paper copy to a light table or window. Tape a 16½" background fabric block symmetrically over the tracing paper copy. With a No. 3 hard pencil trace the design onto the fabric. The design should be easily seen through the fabric. The No. 3 hard pencil lines will be washable.

MAKING A BIAS APPLIQUE BLOCK

1. *Cut out 16 ½" square blocks of background fabric.*
2. *Transfer the design from tracing paper onto 16½" square block of fabric.*
3. *Cut out chosen print material to the size shown in the pattern of the design. Fit the cut-out print material to the space in the design and baste it to the block. I have selected certain sections to be basted as shown in the pattern design and in my quilt, but you can make your own selections. Do not cover outer lines of the design by basted material because the bias must follow the outer lines.*
4. *Now start to bias applique with the longest prepared bias strip, and start in the middle of the design at a line where the bias is to be in the "under" condition. Extend the bias to the middle of space past the line, so that when sewing is finished, the ends of the bias will be well anchored.*
5. *Pin the bias with ¾" sequin pins, pinning the inside or concave line first. Pin about 3" at a time. With invisible stitches, hand sew the bias to the block and move the pins ahead. I found it easier to pin and sew the inside design line, then sew the outside bias without pinning.*
6. *At crossed lines where the bias will be going "over and under," if the first bias is an "over," leave that part unsewn. However, leave a pin with a colored head there to indicate that when the other bias arrives there, it is to go under. At that time the "over" section is appliqued. Conversely, if the first bias to arrive is an "under" condition, then you sew the bias to the block. This treatment is necessary to preserve the Celtic character of the design. The "condition" alternates continually throughout the whole design.*

7. *Square corners and loops that come to a point should be mitred.*

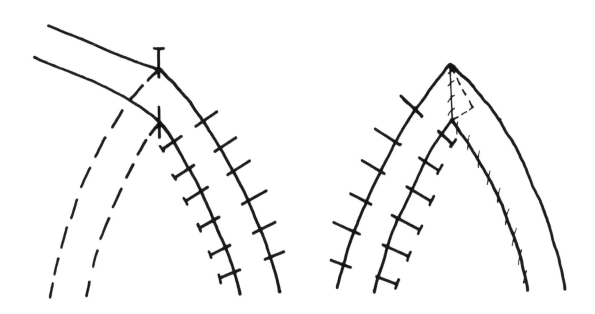

8. *When the bias arrives at the basted cut-out section, proceed as usual using the outer line as a guide. Fit the bias to outside line and pin the inside bias. If the basted material covers a cross section, take extra care at this point. In this case the basted material will be sewn to the block at the same time that the bias is.*
9. *Eventually you will arrive with the bias at the starting point. Since this was an "under" condition, bring the bias through the unsewn section of the other bias, and cut the bias off so that it does not show. Then sew in the "over" section.*
10. *There will be times when the bias is too short. Do not sew two pieces of bias together. Rather, cut off the bias at an "under" section (as described above) and start again with a new piece of bias. Make the bias go from one "under" section to another.*

QUILTING THE QUILT

Use traditional methods for assembling the quilt. After the quilt is assembled and is ready for quilting, just follow the bias stripping with your quilting stitches. If the bias goes "under" at an intersection, make a back stitch, push the needle through and make another back stitch. Start quilting again on the other side. If the bias goes "over," continue quilting as if there was no intersection. When you have finished a block or the quilt, I hope you have the same great feeling I had to see that all the "overs and unders" are just where they should be!

ESTIMATING YARDAGE

Each quilt will vary with size and design and you will need to estimate the number of 16" squares needed for your design. For comparison purposes, I have included the yardage I used for my 90" x 108" Celtic quilt illustrated on the cover of this book.

Background fabric (including backing)	13 yards
Bias strips and strips for garden maze	5 yards
Print inserts	1½ yards
Mountain Mist batting	90" x 108" batt
Thread	over 1000 yards

It is recommended that you wash and dry your fabric before starting. Also, I recommend using 100% cotton for bias, as 50-50 cotton/polyester is more difficult to press. However, it can be used.

May you enter heaven and be presented with all the quilts you were going to do on earth.

Design 1

Design 2

Design 3

Design 4

Design 5

Design 6

Design 7

Design 8

Design 9

Design 10

Design 11

Design 12

Design 13

Design 14

Design 15

Design 16

Design 17

Design 18

16

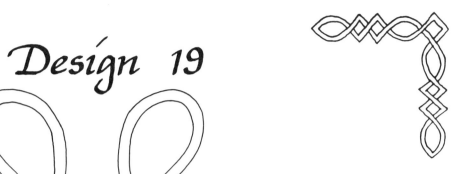

Design 19

Design 20

One-h

← Cut 4 →

design

Cut 4

Design 1

One-half de.

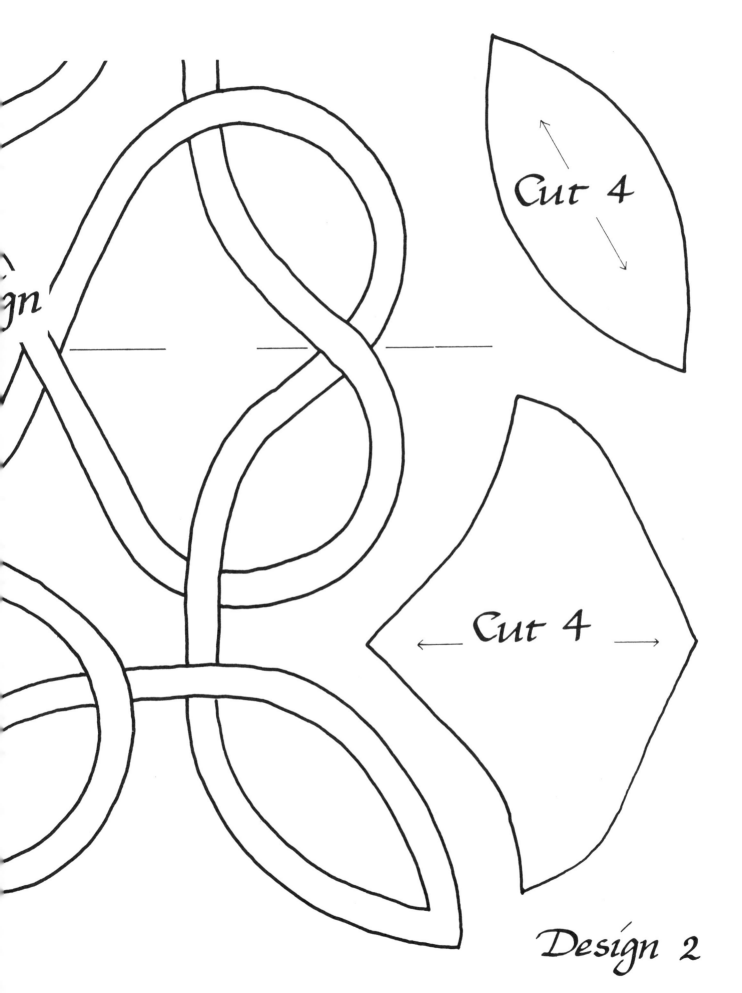

Cut 4

Cut 4

Design 2

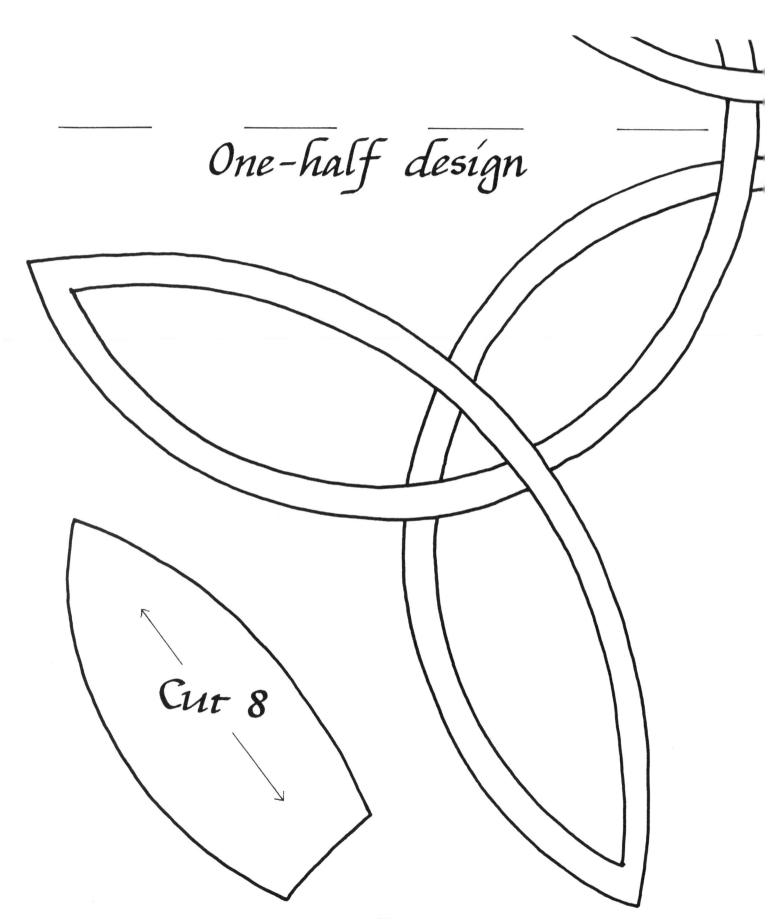

One-half design

Cut 8

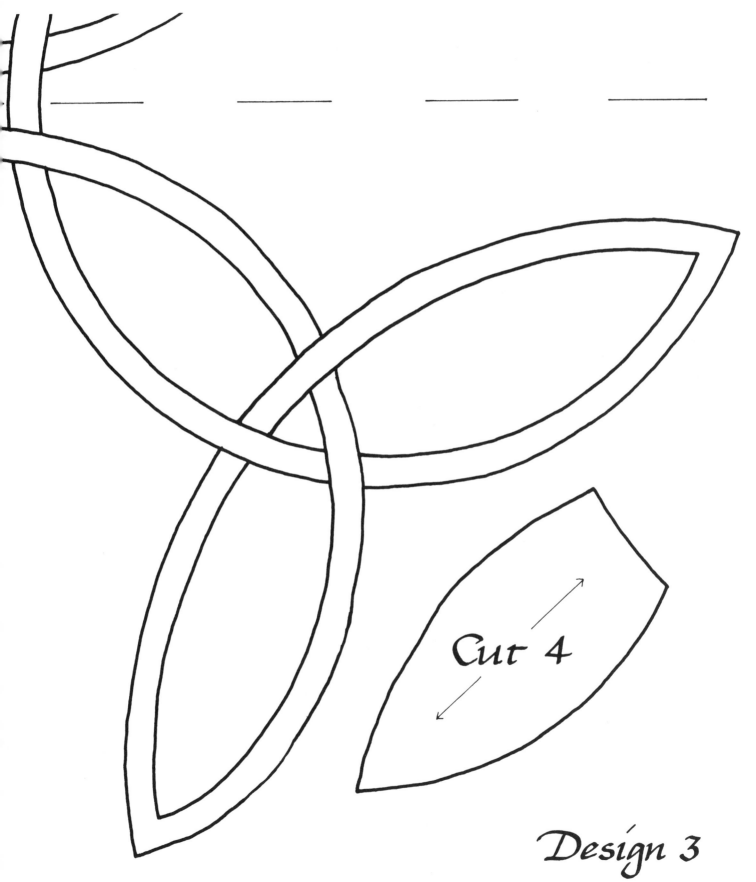

Cut 4

Design 3

One-half design

Cut 4

Cut 4

Design 4

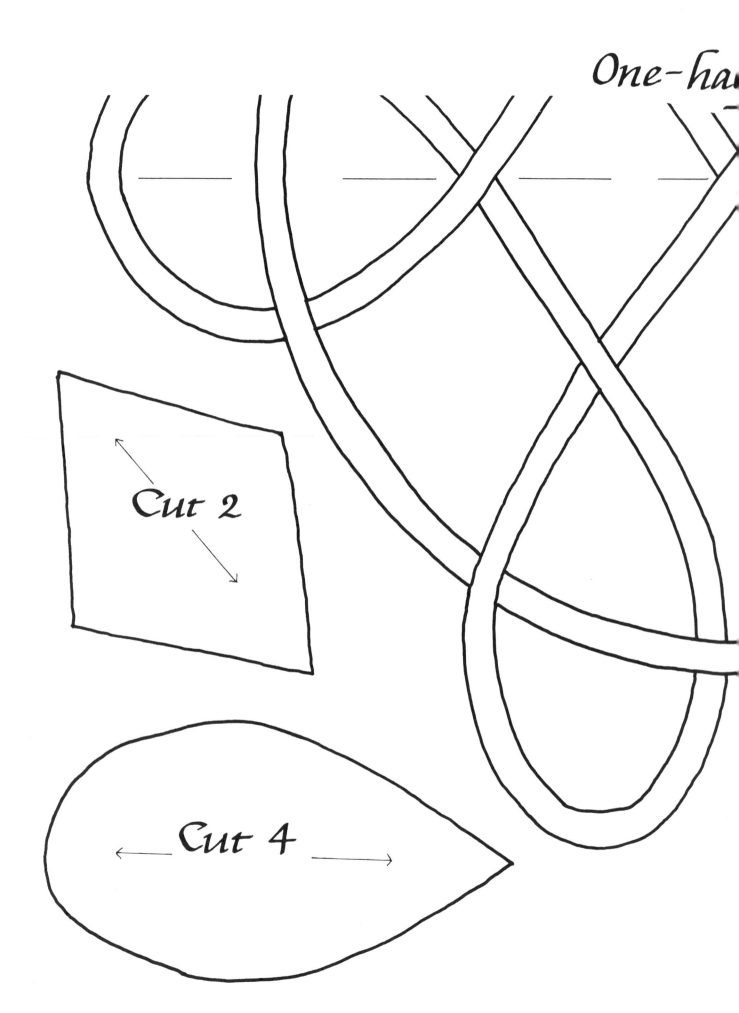

One-ha

Cut 2

Cut 4

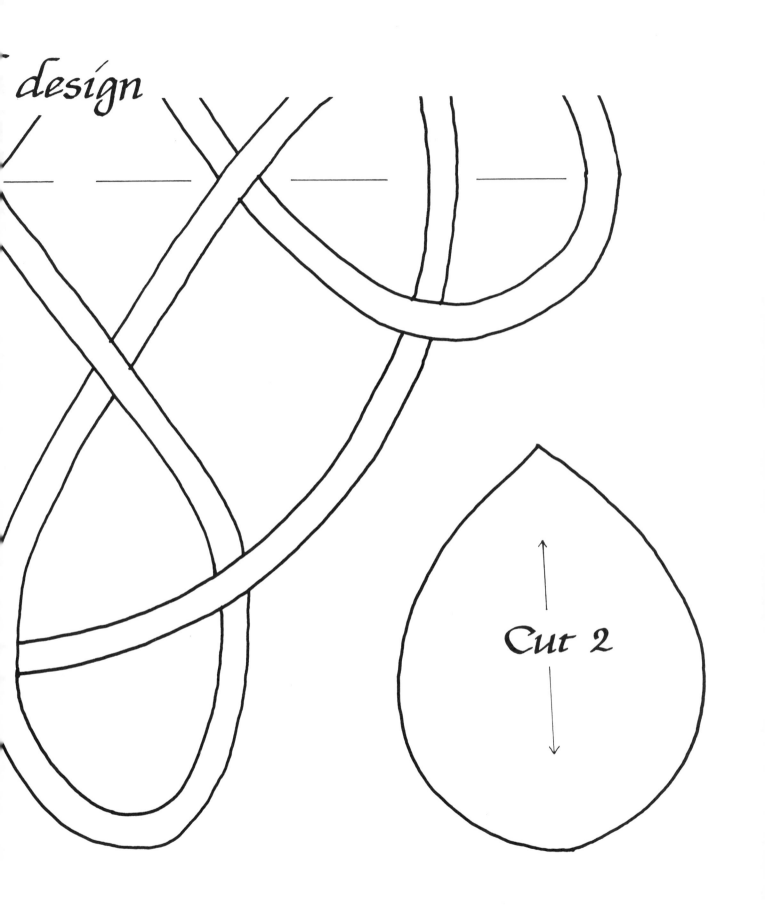

design

Cut 2

Design 5

One-half design

Cut 4

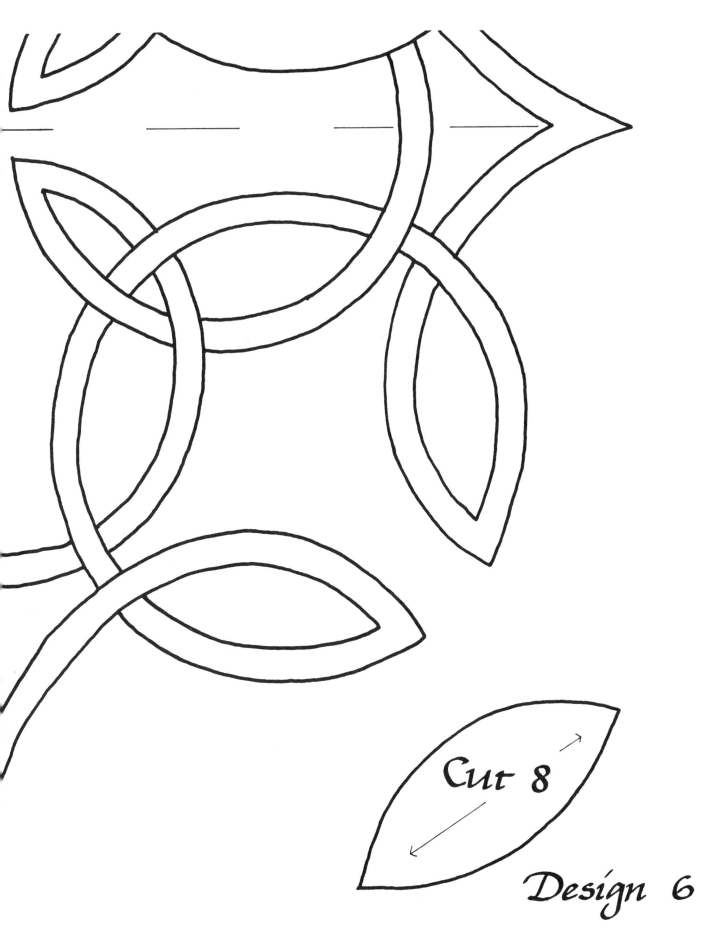

Cut 8

Design 6

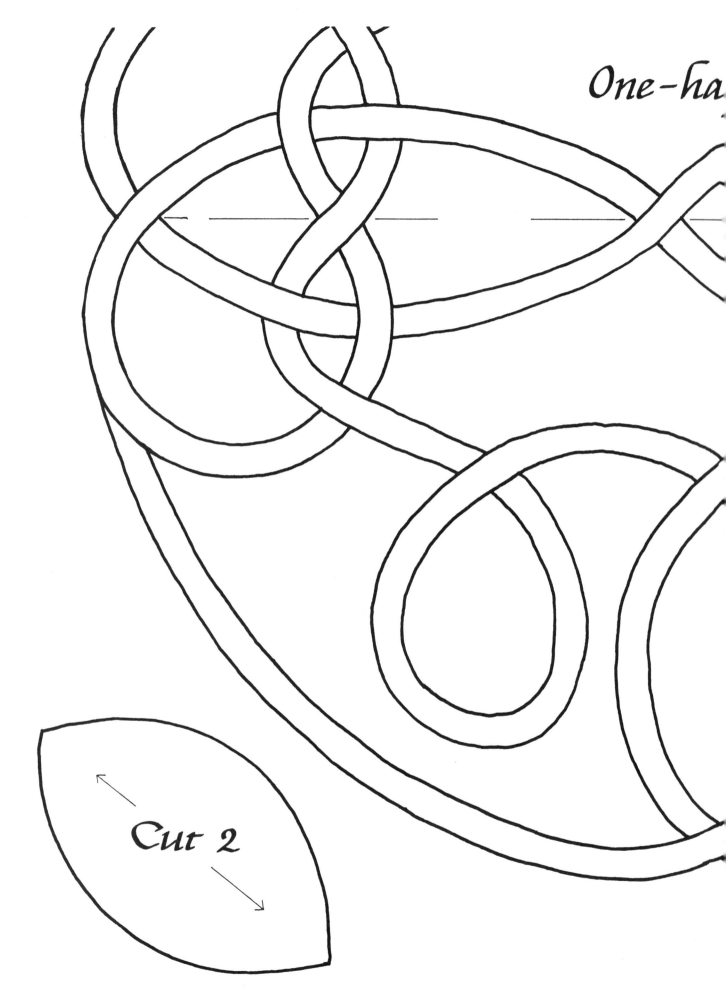

One-ha

Cut 2

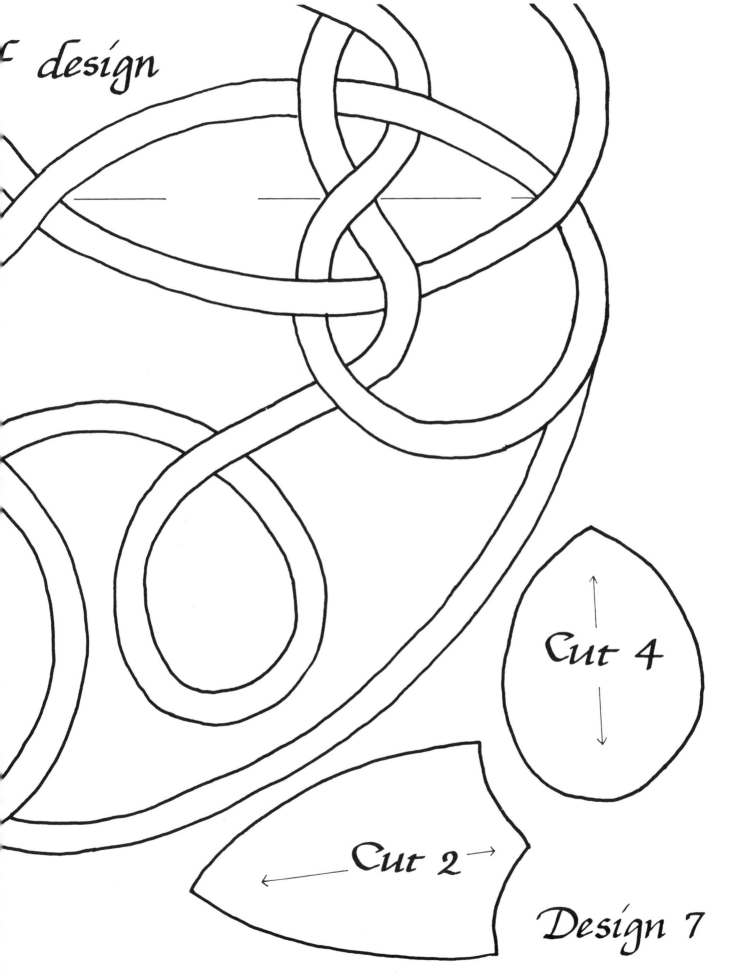

f design

Cut 4

Cut 2

Design 7

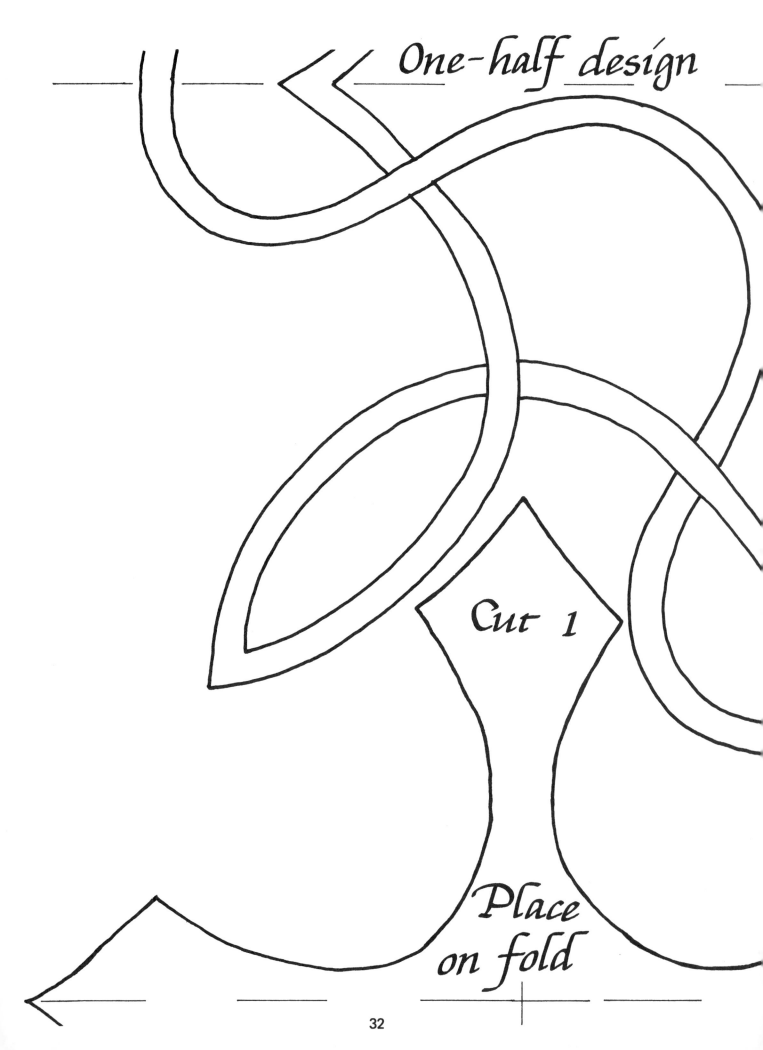

One-half design

Cut 1

Place
on fold

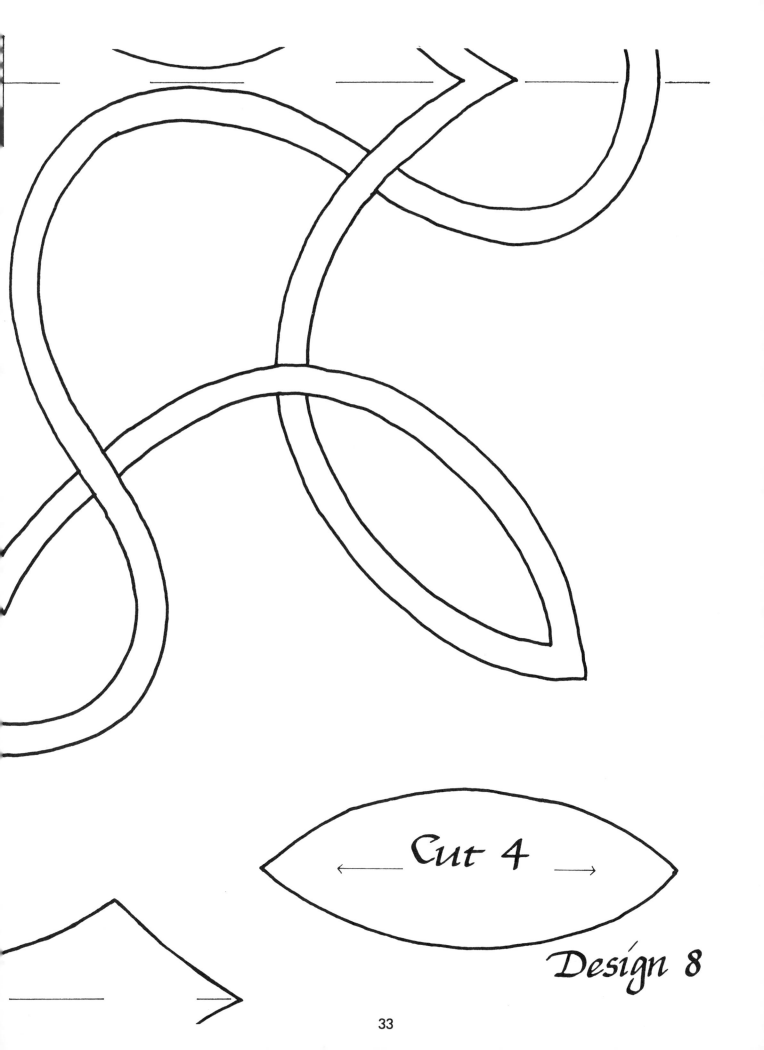

Cut 4

Design 8

ne-half design

Cut 1

Add one-fourth
inch seam

Design 9

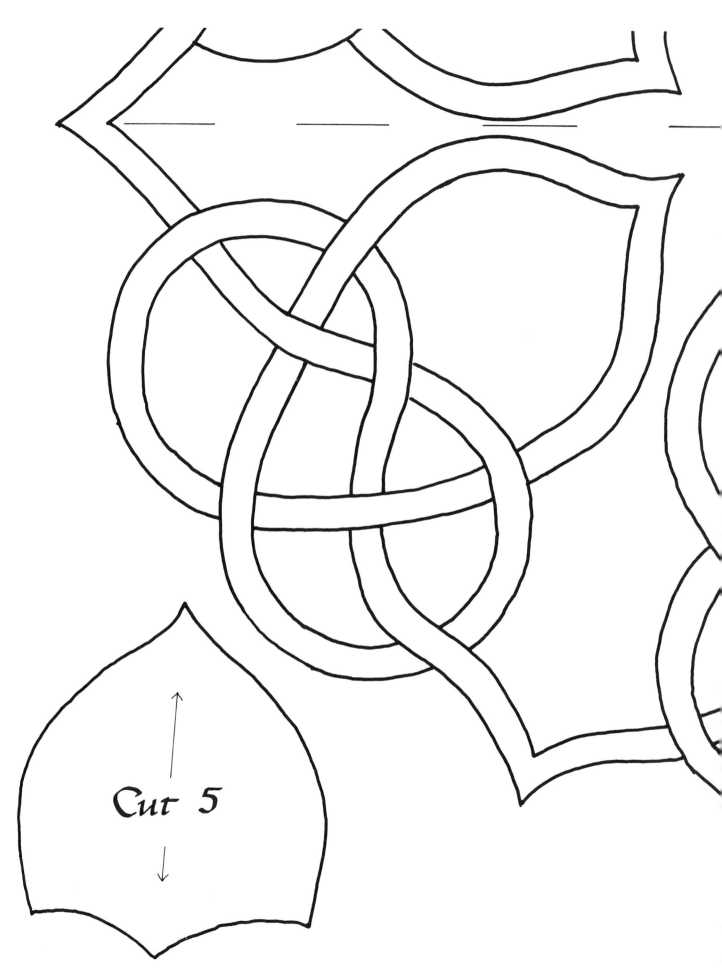

Cut 5

One-half design

Design 10

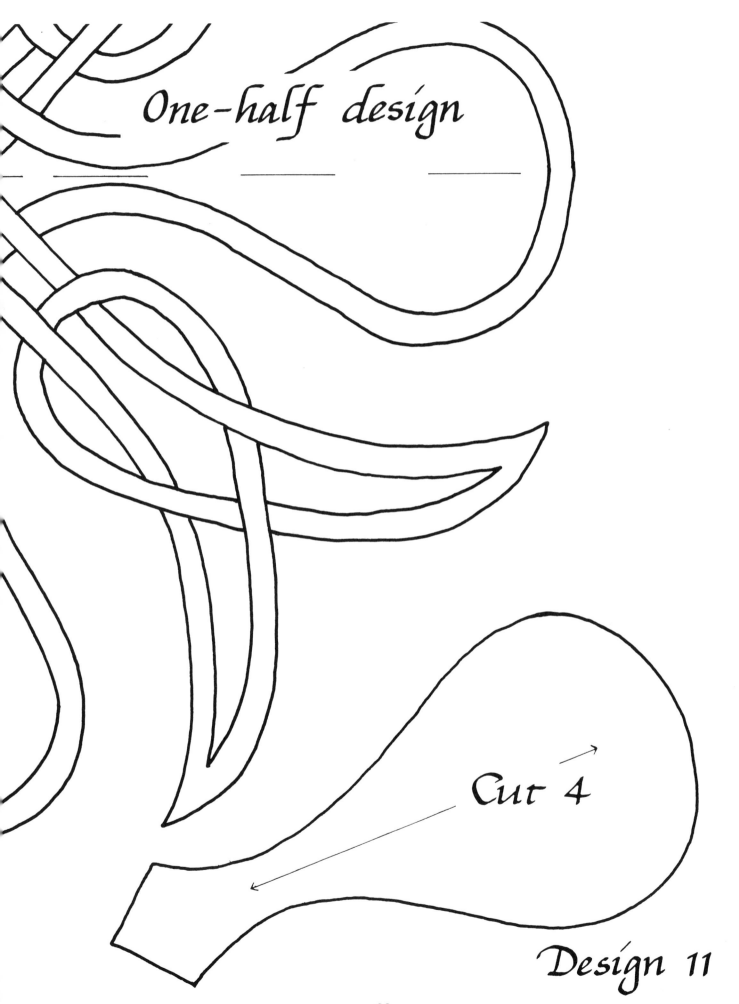

One-half design

Cut 4

Design 11

One-half design

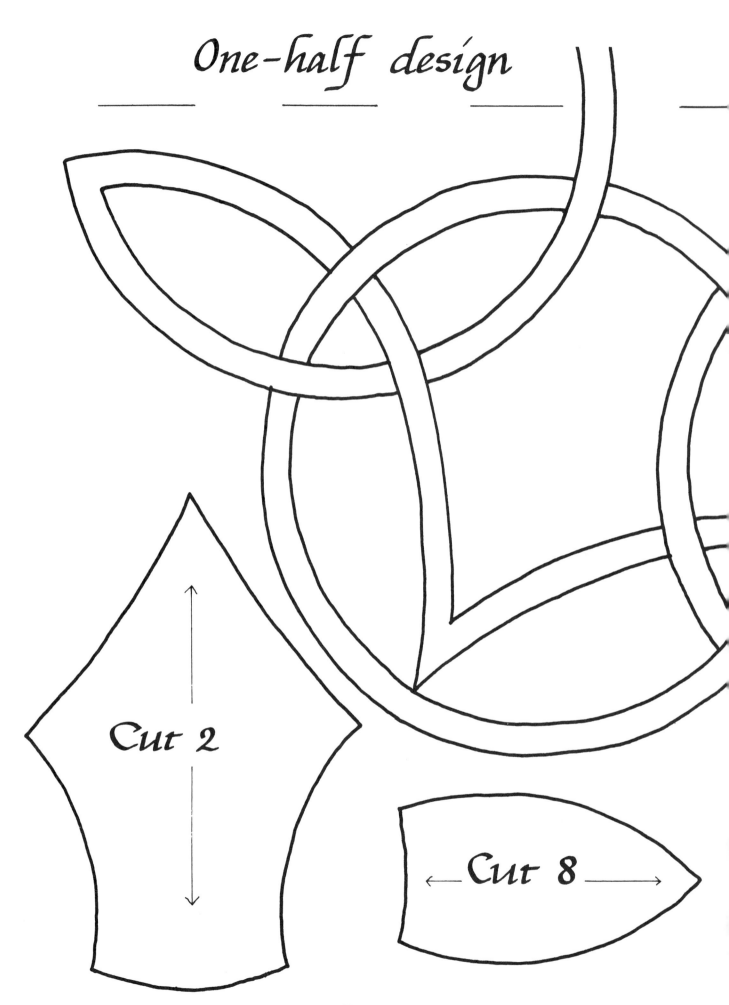

Cut 2

Cut 8

← Cut 2 →

Design 12

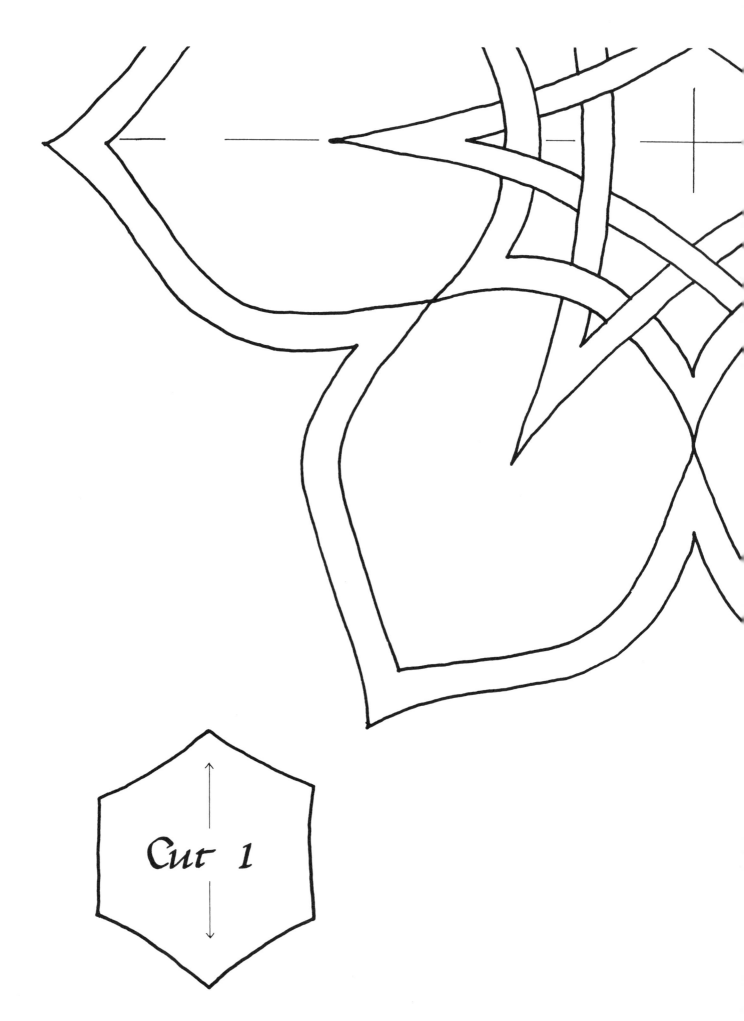

Cut 1

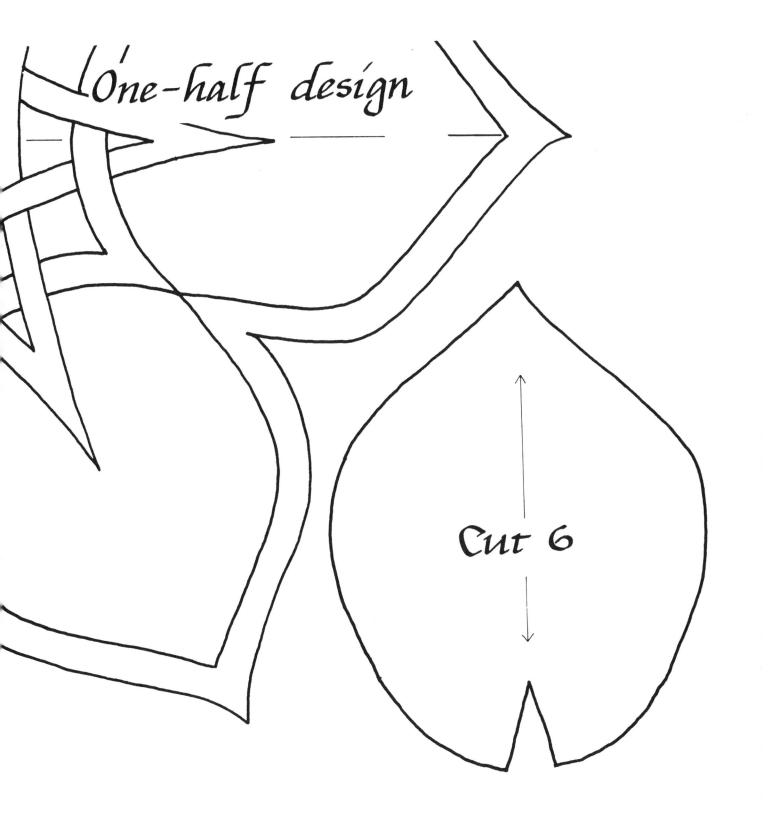

One-half design

Cut 6

Design 13

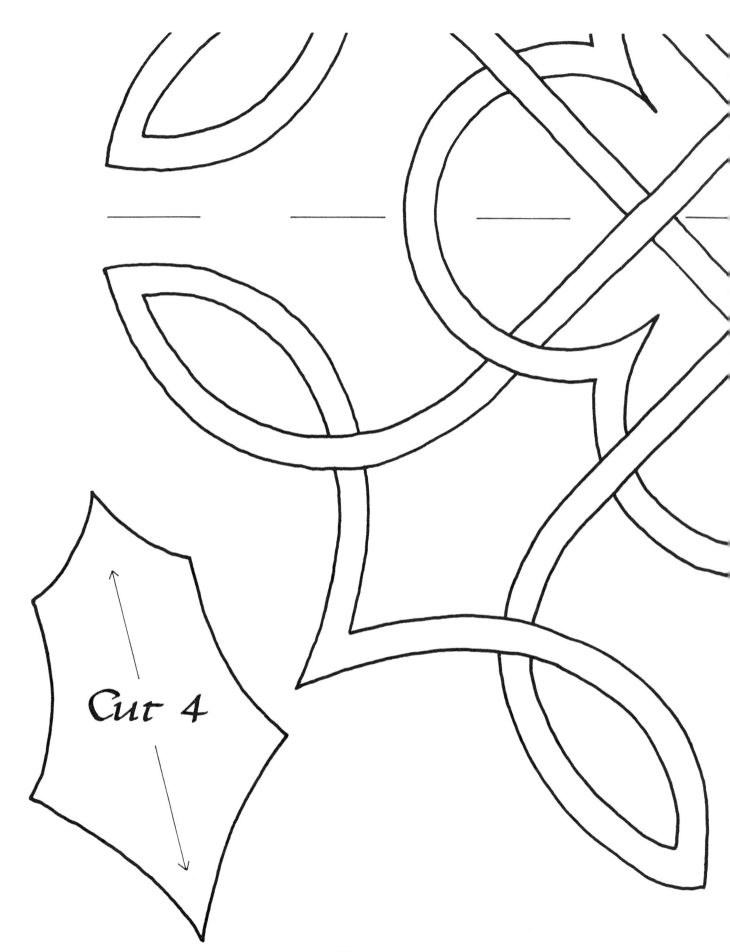

Cut 4

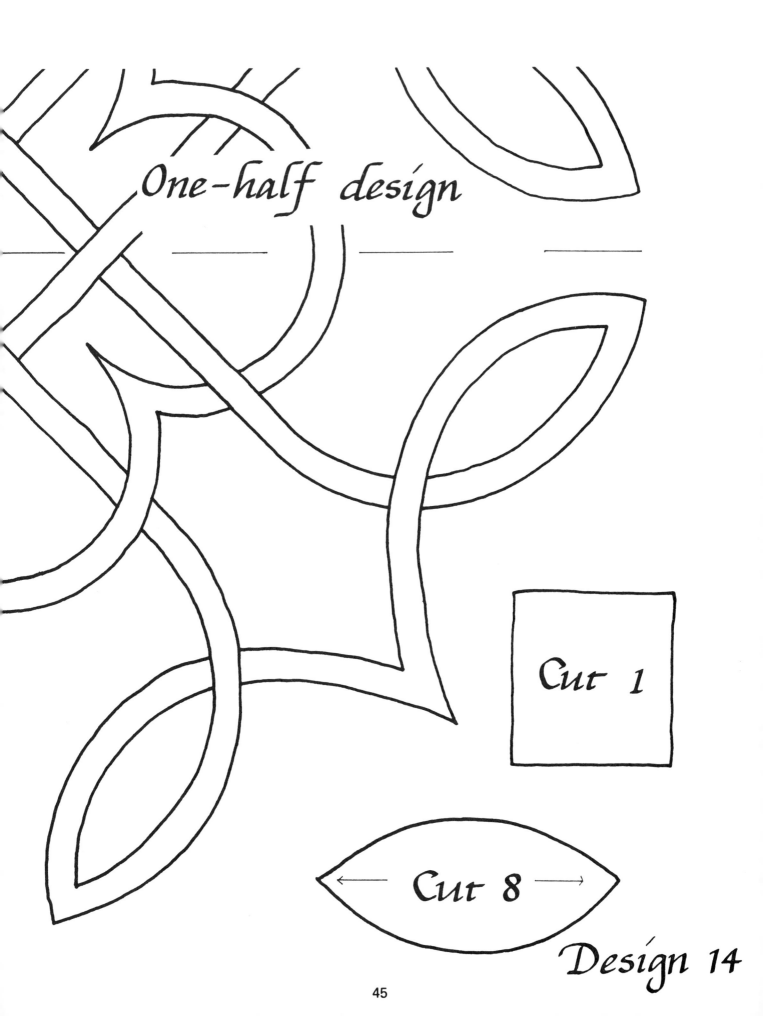

One-half design

Cut 1

Cut 8

Design 14

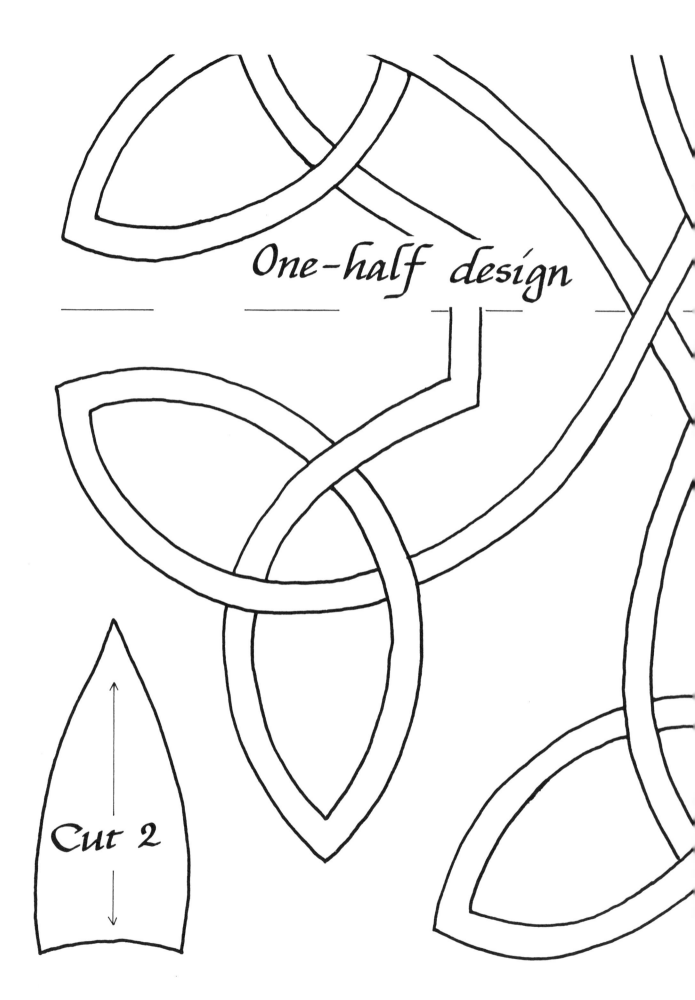

One-half design

Cut 2

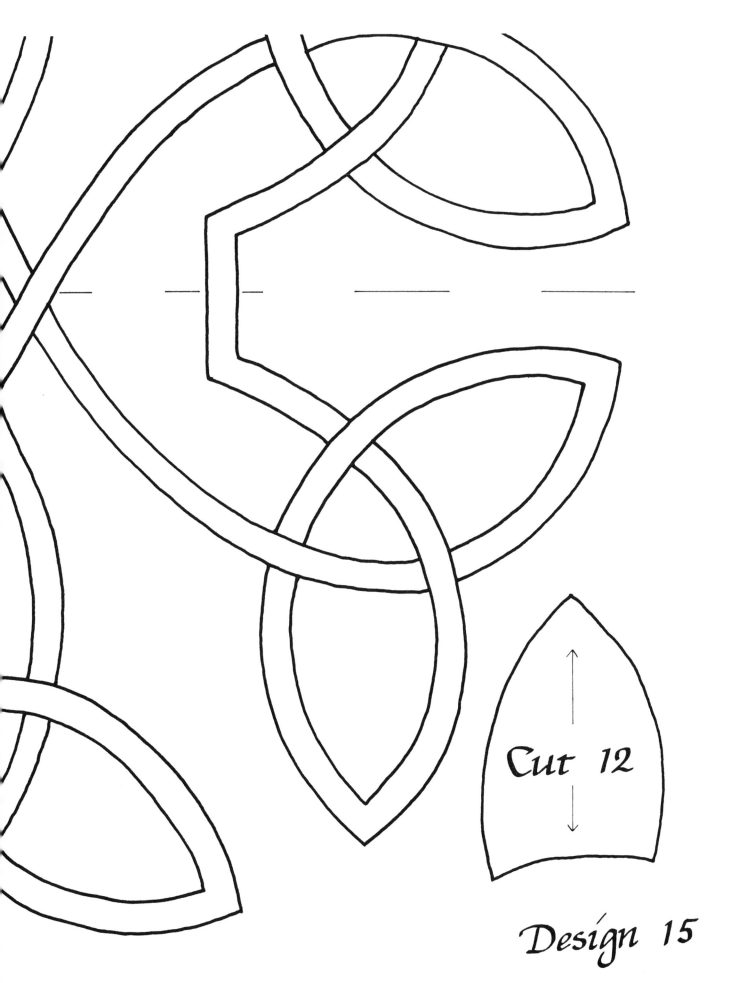

Cut 12

Design 15

One-half design

Cut 1
Add one-fourth
inch seam

Design 16

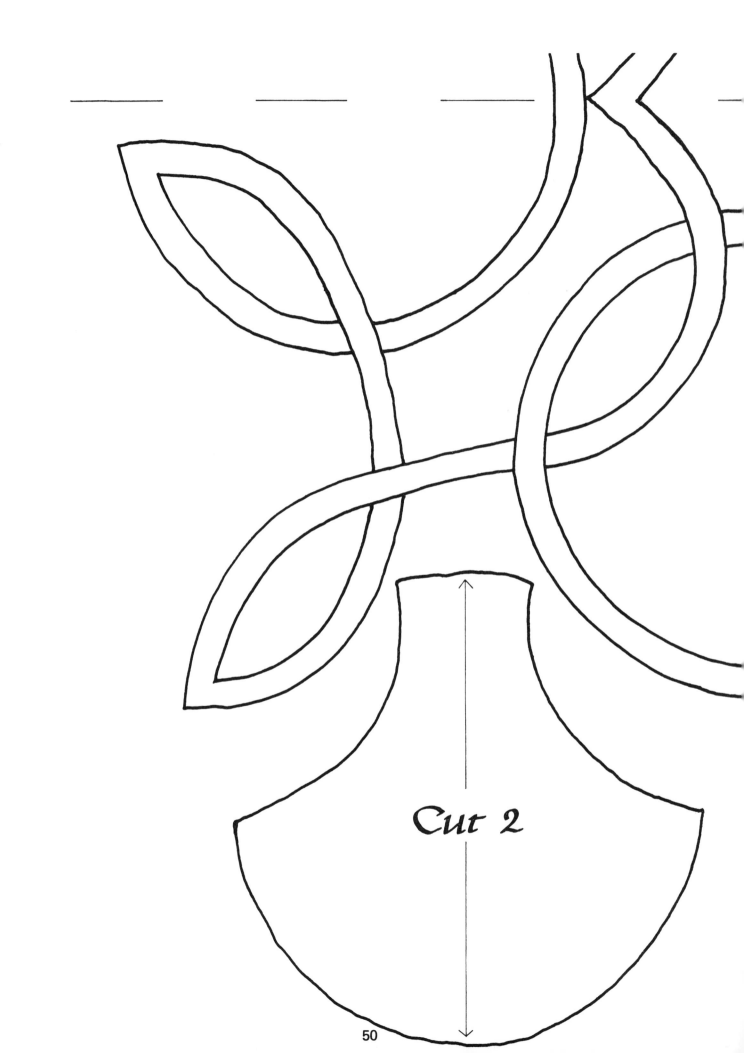

Cut 2

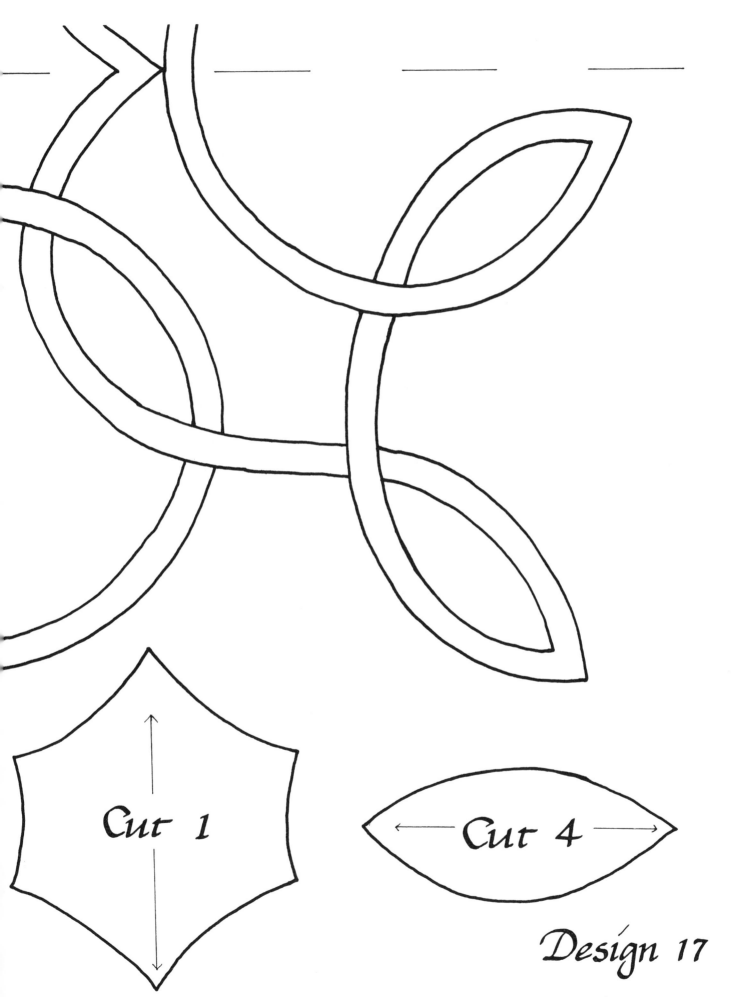

Cut 1

Cut 4

Design 17

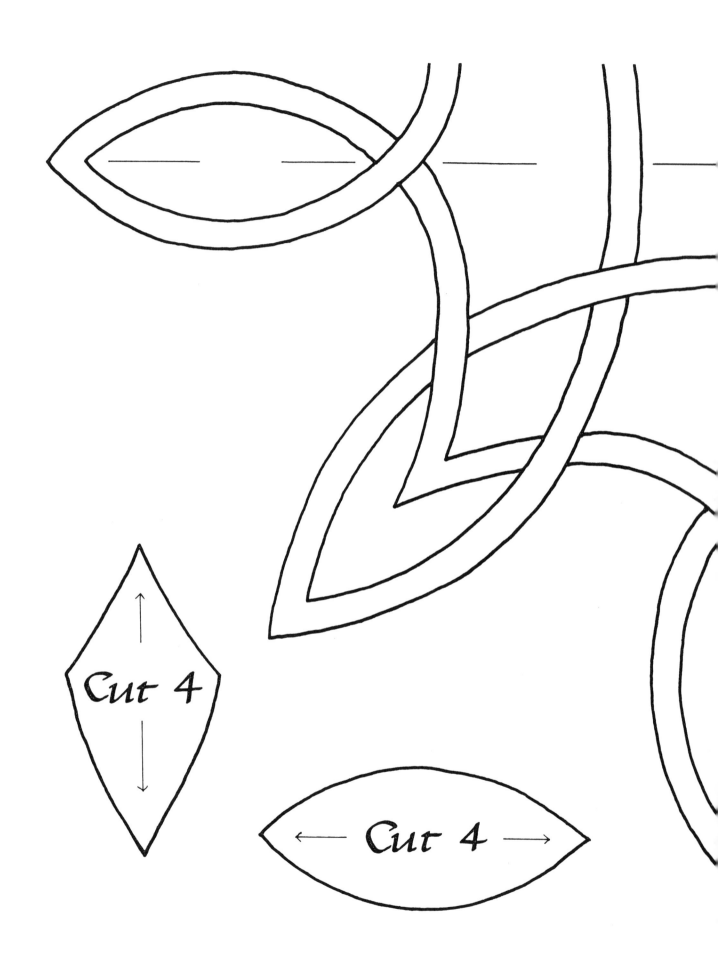

Cut 4

Cut 4

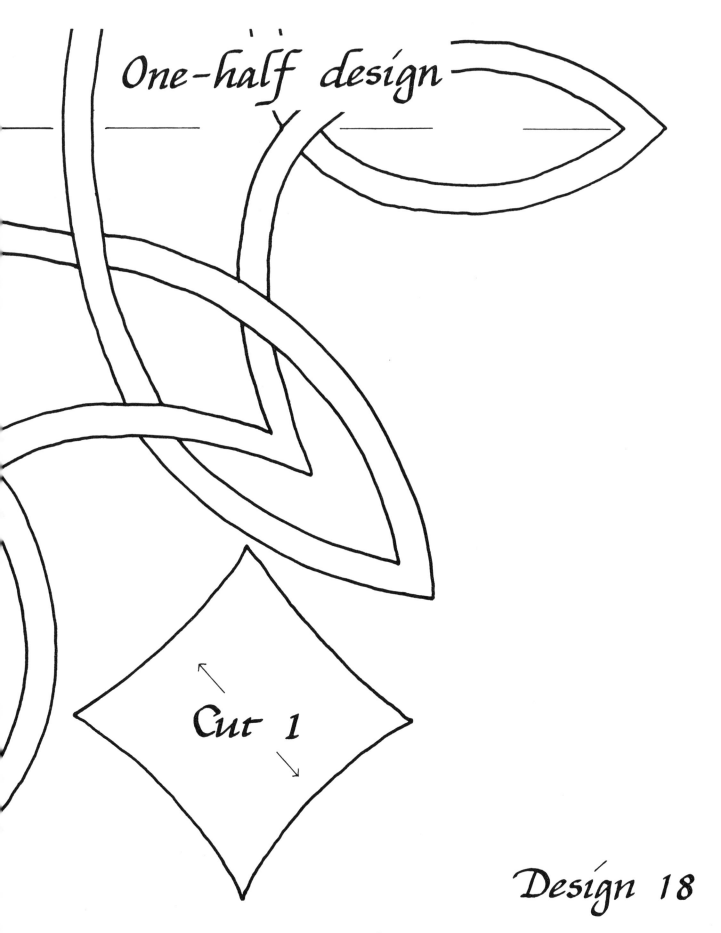

One-half design

Cut 1

Design 18

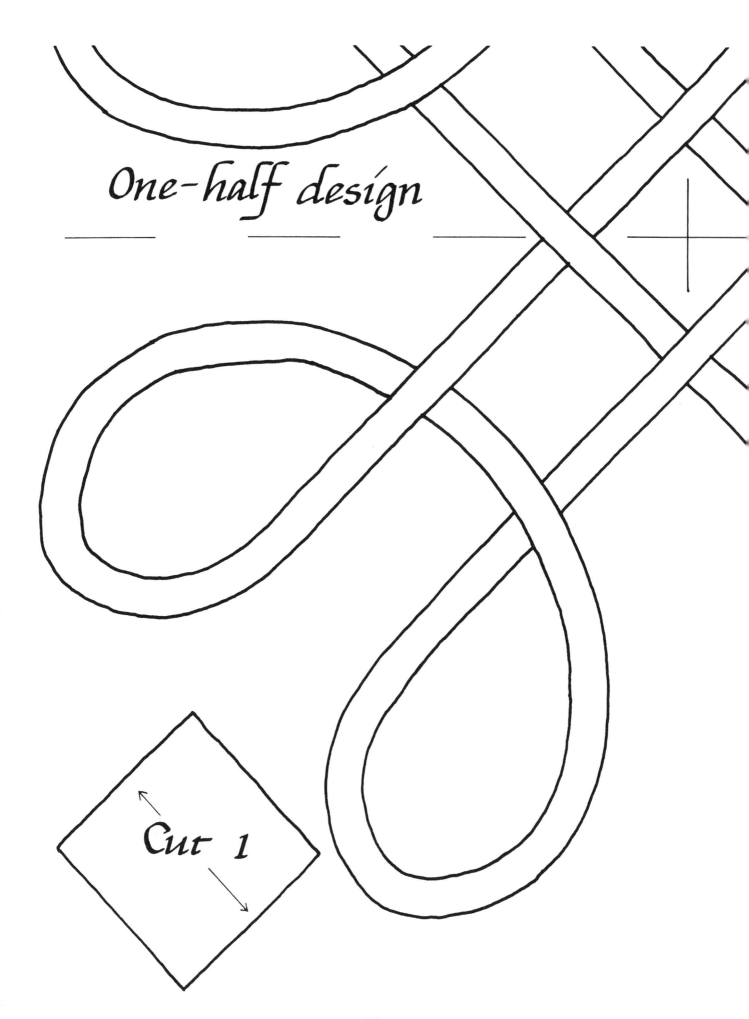

One-half design

Cut 1

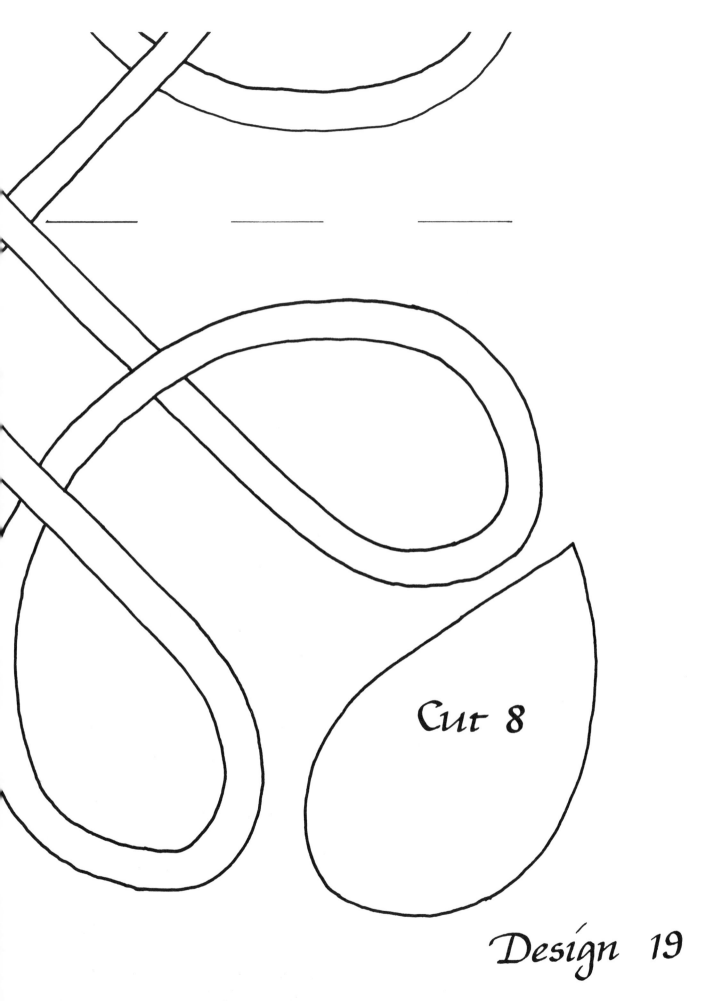

Cut 8

Design 19

One-half design

Cut 8

Cut 4

Design 20

Border

Designs

Acknowledgment

With the friendly help of the following people this book finally got finished;

Marilyn Heyman, calligrapher,

Ginni Berg,

Sylvia Moore,

Marmie Schraub,

Patsy Beattie,

Margret McNall,

Elisabeth (Jake) Feinler,

my husband, Walt,

Bibliography

Book of Kells, Reproduction, Alfred A. Knopf, New York

Bain, George, *Celtic Art*, Dover Publications, Inc. New York

Nordenfalk, Carl, *Celtic and Anglo-Saxon Painting,* George Braziller, New York

Mitchell, F. G.; Harbison, P.; De Pator, L.; De Pator, M.; Stalley, R.A.; *Treasures of Irish Art,* Alfred A. Knopf, New York

Available from the Celtic Design Co.

Bias Bars #1: $1/4$"- $3/8$"- $1/2$" bars

Bias Bars #2: $3/16$"- $5/8$"- $3/4$" bars

Complete Set: #1 and #2 set plus $3/4$" bar

Stencils available for all 20 Celtic Designs featured in this book

Celtic Design Co.

834 W. Remington Dr.,

Sunnyvale, CA 94087.

Printed in China

www.celticquilts.com